BASE
JUMPING

By S.L. Hamilton

VISIT US AT WWW.ABDOPUBLISHING.COM

Published by ABDO Publishing Company, 8000 West 78th Street, Suite 310, Edina, MN 55439. Copyright ©2010 by Abdo Consulting Group, Inc. International copyrights reserved in all countries. No part of this book may be reproduced in any form without written permission from the publisher. A&D Xtreme™ is a trademark and logo of ABDO Publishing Company.

Printed in the United States of America, North Mankato, Minnesota.
102009
012010

PRINTED ON RECYCLED PAPER

Editor: John Hamilton
Graphic Design: Sue Hamilton
Cover Design: John Hamilton
Cover Photo: Getty Images
Interior Photos: Alamy-pgs 6, 7, 10, 11 & 32; AP-pgs 12, 13, 19, 20, 21, 26 & 27; Corbis-pg 26; Daniel Mayer-pg 13; Getty Images-pgs 1, 4, 5, 8, 9, 14, 15, 16, 17, 18, 19, 22, 23, 24, 25, 27, 30 & 31; iStockphoto-pgs 2 & 3; Stuart Ecob-pgs 28 & 29.

Library of Congress Cataloging-in-Publication Data

Hamilton, S.L., 1959-
  Base jumping / S.L. Hamilton.
      p. cm. -- (Xtreme sports)
  Includes index.
  ISBN 978-1-61613-001-5
  1. Jumping--Juvenile literature. I. Title.
  GV529.H36 2010
  796.04'6--dc22

                              2009034939

BASE

"If at first you don't succeed,
well, so much for BASE jumping."

JUMPING

BASE jumpers drop from a fixed point. This might be a mountaintop or a high building.

"BASE" stands for the places where a person may jump:

B = Building

A = Antenna

S = Span (bridge)

E = Earth

JUMP

treme Fact

In 2004, Malaysia held the first BASE jumping competition at the Petronas Twin Towers, which stand an astounding 1,482 feet (452 m) tall.

"B" is for Building

The "B" in BASE stands for Building. A building needs to be at least 50 stories high for BASE jumping. This gives jumpers enough free-fall time to open their parachutes safely. New York City has a number of these tall skyscrapers. But, because of the danger to jumpers and the people below, BASE jumping is not allowed in the city.

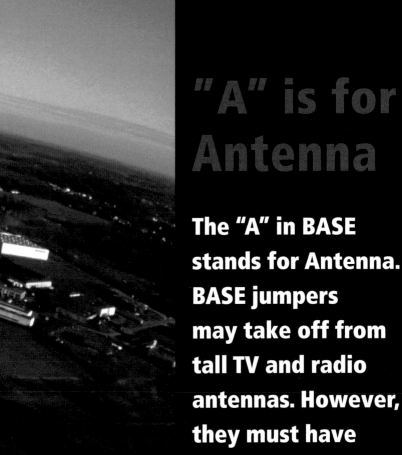

"A" is for Antenna

The "A" in BASE stands for Antenna. BASE jumpers may take off from tall TV and radio antennas. However, they must have permission from the owners to do this.

"S" is for Span

The "S" in BASE stands for Span. This is a natural or man-made object that goes across a deep opening in the earth. Idaho's Perrine Bridge is a popular span. It is 486 feet (148 m) above the Snake River. In 2006, Dan Schilling set a world record, leaping off the bridge 201 times in 24 hours.

Xtreme Fact

BASE jumpers can leap from Idaho's Perrine Bridge at any time of year without a permit.

"E" is for Earth

The "E" in BASE stands for Earth. A jump from a cliff, or other rocky outcropping, gives BASE jumpers only a few seconds to deploy their parachutes. There is very little time to fix any problems that might happen.

After 12 seconds of
falling, BASE jumpers reach
a maximum speed of
119 miles per hour (192 kph).
They cover 175 feet per second
(53 meters per second).
As of mid-2009, 133 people
have died while
BASE jumping.

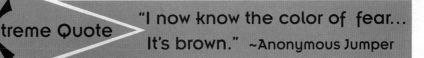

Xtreme Quote

"I now know the color of fear...
It's brown." ~Anonymous Jumper

THE

Xtreme Fact

The National Park Service bans **BASE** jumping from El Capitan. **BASE** jumpers are fighting this in court.

HISTORY

The first modern BASE jump took place in 1966. Skydivers Michael Pelky and Brian Schubert parachuted off Yosemite National Park's 3,000-foot (914-m) El Capitan rock formation. They lived, but both suffered broken bones.

Carl Boenish

Filmmaker and skydiver Carl Boenish is called the "father of modern BASE jumping." Boenish came up with the term "BASE." He also started awarding people with BASE numbers. To be "numbered," a person must jump from each of the four BASE objects. Carl was BASE number 4. His wife, Jean, was number 3.

Carl Boenish died BASE jumping in Norway in 1984.

Most BASE jumpers use a
rectangular parachute called
a canopy. When jumpers pull
the ripcord to open their canopies,
a small pilot chute comes out first.
The pilot chute helps pull out the canopy.

Pilot Chute

Wingsuit

Some BASE jumpers wear wingsuits. This special jumpsuit is designed to catch the air and give lift to the wearer or "pilot." Pilots use their body positions to control where they are going, and how fast. The goal is to drop slowly, so the jumper can enjoy the free fall as long as possible.

Xtreme Fact

Wingsuits are also called birdman or squirrel suits.

Harness, Container, & Helmet

The harness wraps around the body and holds the container. The container looks like a backpack, but holds a BASE jumper's canopy, or parachute. A BASE harness/container gives a jumper some protection. A helmet, sturdy shoes, and knee pads protect the body from hard landings.

"Most bones heal, but few people recover from skull damage." ~BASEwiki on Helmets

WORLDWIDE

Brazil

China

Madagascar

Switzerland

STUNT?

Is BASE jumping an extreme sport or just a death-defying stunt? Many things can go wrong. Parachutes don't open, or open too late. A jumper gets snagged, and then slams into a cliff or other object. Some jumpers have drowned after making a water landing and becoming trapped under their parachute. BASE jumping is one of the most dangerous activities anyone can do.

BASE Number
When a person has jumped from all four BASE obstacles (Building/Antenna/Span/Earth), they may apply for a BASE number. Less than 1,500 people have gotten BASE numbers.

Canopy
Another name for the main parachute that BASE jumpers use.

Free Fall
The time after a person jumps into open air, and gravity begins to pull them down toward Earth, but before the drop is slowed by a device, such as a parachute.

National Park Service
A government agency that is in charge of the national parks in the United States.

Pilot Chute

The smaller parachute that is released first when a ripcord is pulled. The pilot chute, which is attached to the main parachute, enters the airstream first. It is quickly dragged out into the airstream, and helps pull out the bigger main canopy.

Ripcord

A string that is pulled to release a parachute.

Skydiver

A person who jumps out of an airplane with a parachute.

Stunt

An often dangerous, life-threatening activity that requires specific physical skills, strength, and daring.